I0436853

Opinions on America

A Layman's View in Laymen's Terms

Sonny Street

authorHOUSE®

AuthorHouse™
1663 Liberty Drive, Suite 200
Bloomington, IN 47403
www.authorhouse.com
Phone: 1-800-839-8640

First published by AuthorHouse 3/5/2009

ISBN: 978-1-4389-5624-4 (sc)

Library of Congress Control Number: 2009901255

Printed in the United States of America
Bloomington, Indiana

This book is printed on acid-free paper.

Dedication

This book is dedicated to my great granddaughter Breanna Thomas whom I love as "Big As The Sky".

When she is ready to have a family I hope the world will be a better place to live and the love in the world will be as "Big as The Sky"

Acknowledgement

This is to acknowledge my best friend and loving wife. I say thank you so very much for your dedication to me.

I can never put into words and describe my feelings and the humility I feel for your tireless efforts in assisting me in my writing.

Contents

Preface

I have never met a spoiled American. I have only met persons who were born to freedom, in freedom, and of freedom.

Many times I have heard that as an American we are spoiled compared to those who live outside the borders of our country. I have heard now, as an American, there is a tendency to feel we can do anything we want, anytime we want, and we can go anywhere we want. If this is true, then so be it. We are people born into freedom first, and then we're recognized as being from the country of America. America is a place where the people themselves create their destiny. It is a baptism of experimentation into the often misunderstood word of choice.

In this state of freedom, we, as Americans, feel it pulsating through our thoughts, our actions, and our emotions. What we take for granted that is often stated to us is our individual ability to accept wrong or right and the right to make it right. Thus, it's up to us to make things as best we can or better.

Freedom is elusive in that one can earn a million dollars and yet be free as a bum.

We have a pronounced ideology of never wanting to look back, but when we do, we want to make things better through the aggravation that our wrongs have caused.

We seem to approach things in a very loose, investigative way, but once we discover its worth, we pursue it with a very high degree of aggressiveness to prove a point.

Our ability to cope surpasses any individual country's ideology of who we are as a people. No country to date can really put their ideology up against a determined American. As Americans, we strive against ourselves, which makes us better to strive against our enemies.

We even surprise ourselves at the control we have when under pressures or political differences. We seem to have a built-in respect for the Constitution of these United States although many times, we, as Americans, beat ourselves down emotionally in our search for answers that, in fact, show us our own dirty laundry.

If we are poor, we are proud. If we are middle of the road, we are proud. If we are rich, we are proud. There is no level we can reach where pride of who we are doesn't come to the surface.

We are tribal in nature, and this seems to be inherited into our historical heritage of what our nationality is, our nation of origin, and from what part of that nation our origin originated. We are a diversified people among our own nationalities.

We are quick to show our disdain toward tribal traditions and beliefs, but we are also agreeable to change and accept our differences. In our acceptance of differences, we reflect an attitude of, "If I had to go through it, then you do, too." It's the feeling of free choice with competitiveness that actually pushes those who are looked upon as different in the level of equality. It is those who create the demand of recognition for equality that make us realize our own frustrations and our own disbelief in how we are raised to believe. How dare they! A sound appreciation evolves us as Americans from the disbeliefs and frustrations.

Aging

At sixty-five, I laugh to see my age made fun of.

I feel pride when I see my age given respect. I sadden to see my age demeaned. I cry to be called old, and all because at my age we are mature. Do we have more common sense at maturity or just a mellow understanding of everything? Why has old been attached to humanity when all the mature knowledge together can create more into life?

True love is when two mature adults can hug and cry from it, pushed by emotional holidays of life reflected, called the "Old Days." Tears of joy are the blood of true love.

There is always a reasoning of foreshadowing in death, so why is the reason always supernatural? We seem only to notice after death the situation of odd events; then we blend them into the death and say "How odd."

Pain can subside while emotionally it lives forever.

Heartache hurts forever.

Loss is timely.

Memories are only put into time; reflection brings it back at times.

Being a grandparent is the last redemption at showing your kids you raised them right.

Grandkids are everything you wanted your children to be.

Great-grandkids are made students of the reality of why great-grandparents are to be respected.

Great-grandkids are that part of the cycle of life that brings the final touches of legacy to the grandparent and the final try at accumulating love, memories, and the sanctifying end to life with grace and humility.

Being grandparents represents all the right times you didn't have for your own children as you were busy raising the total life of the family.

Health

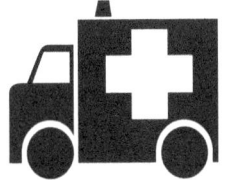

There should be no politics when it comes to the health of our elderly who built this nation.

National health homes should be built to house our aging and care for them with dignity.

To be ill and disabled in our society today is to be shown as different.

Illness seems to be something of suspicion or something that we should run from as a burden.

Family members run from debilitating long-term illness after an attempt to rationalize the length of time spent.

Our government runs from long-term illness and only tempers it with long-term political promises that fade like the victims of illness.

When elderly people receive their Social Security card, they become a profit to the medical field. Look at the immense cost of drugs.

The old days are a sign of times for all ages.

Hospitals become strictly business when you die or when Medicare can no longer pay as you start becoming an invalid. Rest homes are hospital outs. You might as well be dead when a hospital no longer can care.

This may be the only country where elected officials get a better health insurance plan than the people who elected them.

Devastating illnesses mean devastating

financial liability in an equal society. How devastating!

The profit in pharmaceuticals is the political action of this nation.

Why has the hypocritical oath become a position of health insurance?

Elderly persons pay more for their health insurance programs and prescription drugs while the young with the same ailments pay less.

Since when does a pill and treatment

change its cure with age?

Drug company profits will always outlive the elderly as it addicts them to live at any cost.

Possibly some of our congressmen and senators are not fighting the real war on drugs, as they may be pandering their positions in politics based on drug company donations.

You know you are elderly when you can hardly find a store today that has your style of clothing. These are the same stores that you purchased from when you were young and growing older.

When dialing a phone to an HMO or hospital, an elderly person who has arthritic hands, is tone deaf and lacks instant memory is expected to make an appointment without difficulty from a menu that switches departments in a heartbeat. It's worse when the person you find yourself talking to has a heavy foreign accent you cannot understand even when you may have excellent hearing.

Parents

Parents always seem to tell their children where they are at and not how they got here.

All children are blameless until they commit a wrong in sex or crime. Yet, no one will start a child's education on these subjects until it is a dominating, confused factor of religious commitment or biased education.

Education starts in a child as a mother's emotional feeling. Why does it stop at the first breath of life by putting an age factor on the born child?

Americans' fascination with guns seems to forget our children. Why do schools not teach the history and safety of guns to our children?

Our schools lay quietly at the death toll of gun accidents to our children. This is our real education from our ignorance.

Parenting love is not DNA. It is being a real parent. Our courts use mixed standards to destroy the strongest connection of this bonding between a person and a child. They use biology, which has nothing to do with parenting love.

Good parents are smart, covert operatives in their children's growing lives.

A child is a reflection of its parents' past that improves on its children's future.

Inconsiderate parents are those who let their children scream and whine in public places, thus taking away the rights of those who watch in disbelief. The parents, not the child, should be slapped into reality for robbing the rights of others, especially by the elderly whose nerve endings must be at skin level in aging respectfully.

Discipline is an act of peer pressure and social structures, which evolves into respect. It is not a psychological phase of doing your own thing.

A child's question of, "Are we there yet?" is important to all in the listening distance.

A small child's love is pure.

A baby's love is life.

A grown child's love is respect and understanding.

Holidays are of mixed emotions.

Birthdays are emotional.

Death is expected only after it happens.

Why is an "Owee" the most explained pain in our life as a child? Could it be as parents we take it into ourselves?

Education

A total education solves even the smallest questions outside the realm of the education system itself. No problems can be resolved without personal education in a group or by an individual.

Education gives a better understanding of all life. Maturity is wiser though it mellows in every aspect that life bestows on its age. Second to that is knowledge with its age.

Universities are a black hole of spending on those in favorite positions of prestige.

The reality of the university is the professor and student. They alone question *the questions of the totality of life, with discipline and thought, and then answer with more questions that are ongoing.*

High schools are unworkable euphoric dreams of past matured students for their missed puberty of popularity.

The only war America is really losing is in the education equality of her grammar and high school youth.

Dropouts always have their reasons, while the education system has its blindness to become educated by the frustration of the dropout student.

Continuation schools are a repeat of the same problem to the dropout student, so why continue? Dropout students are the next state welfare trainees. If welfare has to train them, then why have continuation schools?

Technical school and career schools are cheaper than special classes, continuation schools and welfare.

Education today goes on and on and on, and nobody seems to catch on to the needs of a system that works for the dropout.

Dropouts are a prisoner of a social system program that lacks in realities of the dropout's needs and ambitions. Education is only the answer when the brain encloses on its needs, rather than a program that demands.

Education in its own right demands discipline. Dropouts have a different type of discipline that is demanding to them, so why hasn't education searched toward those demands outside the box of the education system?

Sex

To be different is to be provocative.

Total satisfaction of body and mind is the total climax of sex.

Sex is a stimulant to the body of life.

Stimulating sex is joyful.

Sex education to a child is not a wrong at any age; it is an education to right.

Morals do not belong in education. Education teaches morals.

The words we define as swearing are expressions used only in variable situations. Yet, the worst words used are any words said in anger.

Sex at its climatic orgasm is pure. Or, is it porno that our kids should not know about?

At the moment of climatic orgasm, are we religious, or are we animals of nature?

Can you ever recall praying at a climatic orgasm when trying to conceive life?

Is it a sin to say, "Jesus Christ," or "Oh, God!" during an orgasm?

Is saying, "Oh, fuck" during an orgasm better than saying, "Oh, God!" or "Jesus Christ?"

Murdering a producer of life is already a crime.

If a woman with a fetus is murdered, how is it considered two murders?

What about the seeds in a man that are called sperm? If he is murdered, is this only one murder or multiple murders? Without one, there is none. So why do we have more laws to protect which is already protected as one? Is there an agenda here?

Women are of nature's giving. Men are of nature's taking.

Men are emotional to the female. This causes the feelings of protection copulation and the sustaining of the animal pride. The family is a continuation of the demand of survival and to a god that may be their implanted belief.

The life equality of both are the position nature has put on them—men being the emotional protector of the life, and women as the strong surviving part of the relationship. They are to maintain the continuing tribal survival to extend the life of earth. Both are important to one another and should never share a dominating role.

Equality

Equality flaws in our society are simple. That part of society that cries the loudest for equality is the loudest in showing our diversity.

Politicians use equality to show how perfectly it can be corrected.

As a society seeking perfection in equality, we perfect a society of difference at the attempt.

Equality is elusive in our society, but only for a name. The named society means a social circle or group of social circles having a clearly marked identity. Yet, we see a constant diversity at the political seeking that of perfection in our system of imperfect democracy. As a democratic system, we lack the definitions to equality. It would seem we are rebellious only when equality is used to notice us.

Equality cannot be found in the Constitution since the Constitution is used to make equality. It needs no defining state of mind; it only needs definition.

Environmental

Environmentalists are a cancer on humanity, unless through strong scientific proof they can stand up and be accounted for in their endeavor to save any species that won't evolve through natural occurrence. Even in their best efforts, evolution is the environmentalists.

The endangered species list is a fraud perpetrated by emotional positioning of political posturing. Now that the importance of the spotted owl is gone, is the list not evolving?

Even after a forest burns, evolution survives. Along with this, the earth ages gracefully. Time is time, and there is no time to change it back.

One thing the environmentalists have done is they've created our environment.

Politics

Education of law creates competitive liars, who in some instances, gain positions of power to write the laws against and into this system of laws. It's done to maintain their own. Look at the retirements of our politicians.

Politics never go to the point at issue; it only circles the individual and protects ignorance of the reality of the issue. Then it maintains that ignorance to the vote. Once voted on, ignorance is no excuse.

The difference between a democrat and a republican is the distance at which they stand facing each other. Otherwise, they both go in the same direction.

Free man will always have a multitude of politics.

To be an independent in politics is a correlation of favors to either side of democrat or republican, and then it questions the revelations of politics.

One can say that the democratic philosophy seems to question the quality of society with a philosophy close to Karl Marx socialism.

The republican philosophy seems to question the equality on issues and its fiscal implications; yet, it is done with a moral stance of religious fervor that almost implies a conflict of church and state.

Political polls are news media's lifeline, but that is another story.

If the general public were asked a serious and true question by pollsters, then maybe we would not need to vote.

Freedom of speech is both conservative and liberal. If we push the limits of freedom of speech in our ideology, we can possibly lose it. Patriotism is our leverage. This is how we know there is more than conservative and liberal politics.

Representation of the voter has never corrected the issues of America. It has only chased its tail in the glory of self.

Poverty in America is elusive and becomes an aggressive tool only when the party that is running for office wants the public to know how bad the party in office is doing. The question is what was the condemning party doing while the poverty was getting worse?

Real political representation would not have the best social benefits for its representatives and unequal benefits for *its poorest constituency. We have a long way to go.*

When politicians put themselves out as common persons of America, should they not be even more common?

There is no politician greater than the fear he holds on public opinion.

To be blindsided is worse than to see it coming, but what hurts more?

Lies are easy when you believe in them. Truths can be turned into lies that are believable.

Exaggeration is neither lies nor truth; it is only a description of either.

How simple are American politics; how frustrating is the control of its ideas.

There is no truth in advertisement because political campaigns would not exist.

A vote is worth more than a dollar of influence. It can replace the influenced.

A recall in politics is a recall of society itself.

Haven't' there been more laws written in control of freedom than in communism?

If we believe in ourselves, why do we have politics to believe?

Politics are the worst course that freedom takes, but because of the vote, it can be somewhat restrained.

Politics are immature in nature as they

evolve into childlike competitiveness; too many choices made by the children of law.

●

We seem to have more government employees in some state governments than regular employees in our markets and industries. Is this due to cuts in their spending?

●

There is no bigger criminal in our government than the INS. The whole program should be deported. Look to our nation's borders.

●

Jane Fonda made herself different; it must have been easy for her or anyone that *represented her to talk with authority in a free society given so many war grave markers. Her patriotism became what can be considered the ultimate use of freedom of expression under provocative action.*

Patriotism can be stupid, but it lives in the hearts of heroes.

Bill Clinton is remembered as the man in office as the president. Monica Lewinski is remembered as the person who brought down the office of the presidency. Two parallels; one place.

There is no right, left, liberal, conservative,

moderate, or centric. It is all acting with words by the freedom of media. In actuality, it is individualism in a final ending to place the vote.

Filibuster to the democrats and republicans means no. Go figure!

Secular ideals may be God-made, but who is to say it's not?

Moral standards are not for government or media to define. They're for the faithful to celebrate and use in their daily lives.

Stem cells and stem cell research are both of God's will. Or, is stem cell research secular and stem cells just that, stem cells? Does anyone have a definition from God as supposedly God created reason and secular after God created cells?

A president said he would not use federal tax dollars for stem cell research, as it is not appropriate. Yet, we put millions into the pockets of our school unions and our school systems that have been destroyed and failing. Is that equal?

All problems that we face as Americans in America are from yesterdays. There has never been a new tomorrow; just death and taxes with the "same old, same old."

The only problem in America that was ever fixed was, and is, in the original documents that created this nation. Since then, interpretation has created the greatest experimentation in freedom and a lot of faults.

Our greatness as a world nation leader is not by the words of our leaders, but by the words we give our leaders from our actions to them. Our resolve is in itself us.

When man can reach beyond the

restrictions placed upon him, then and only then, is he free. Slavery is physical, yet emotions are also slavery.

Women are the mothers of earth. Men are raised by women. So, there is no stupidity between them. Society breeds the stupidity within each gender.

The greatest thing that nature has given to man is a woman who stands by him. The smallest thing is resentment.

To call a re-elected president a liar is to call the people that elected the president liars, and that generally comes from the losers that are less than all the liars combined. It just may be that the losers are lying to themselves.

Are we stupid enough in America to elect a president without experience during a wartime period because of charisma popularity?

Give me a woman president candidate to vote for who has served her nation in uniform, or a strategic position of political power that requires knowing your enemies at arm's length, and it will help America to survive.

Law

The laws written after the Constitution are in many instances challenging to our ideas of freedom.

Abortion will never be a law as it divides. It is more a moral standard and opinion to date.

Our Constitution made us who we are, but we made the Constitution law what it is. Life, liberty, and the pursuit of happiness is the final definition of our choice.

The Constitution is not a perfect document. This must be why it is interpreted in so many legislated ways. The question, then, is with our experiment in freedom.

Is it because we, as a society, want out from under our own Constitution? Or, is it because we are ignorant and blind to what freedom really is? Do we lose the intent of our emotional feeling of freedom within ourselves when we form a group to project outwardly in society those problems? Then, do we watch it change as it gathers various interpretations from other groups, as it becomes a law?

Society cannot determine laws over the Constitution. The Constitution is the rule of law over society. Society becomes emotional toward itself and tries to direct the popularity of that emotion to be above the Constitution, such as racism and sexuality.

The Fifth Amendment in the Constitution is the only lie that exists in the document of restraint. It is a blanket over truth that is made toward the Constitution during its use.

There are many local judges elected to the bench without identity to political affiliation. This seems to show that no law exists to keep equality in the judgment on local levels that are more influential than the judges identified in political affiliation on our highest courts. Is that fair and equal?

Authority is not law; it is a mature knowledge to respect that, which has matured under the laws.

Laws should be written not by lawyers alone or by laymen. They should be written by the ones that hold the most experience to the change.

Remember, a police officer's job must suck, as he never chases a good guy. So how can life be happy for them?

If we, as Americans, took the power of the vote to absolute, then the laws would stay black and white with no gray areas in between. The interpretation of the rule of law would be nonexistent.

Prisons are a place where the system tries to do its best with the worst conditions that help in the lateness of the attempt.

If ignorance of the law is no excuse, then what do we call a lawyer who loses his case?

High Crimes

Why do we always have more media coverage on a criminal CEO than on the lifestyle changes of the victims?

Why is there never an arrest made in government when obvious waste occurs when money disappears, and it's happening at criminal levels that should be prosecuted? The biggest crime after waste is the transferring of the individual to another government position, which sometimes is higher than the first position held by the individual. So, why do we, as a voting society, vote the individual's bosses back into power?

Any concentration of positions of power, large or small, creates control and dominance with a lot or little larceny. Most high-level crime can be found in power, and most awarded power is high-level crime.

We have no kings or queens in our society, but most high-level CEOs or judicial appointees who commit crimes are treated with royalty and sent to domains apart from what they really are as criminals. Their restitution, as it is called, is made at model prisons that look like Sunday schools compared to the namesake they are called as criminals. The words prison and common criminals become blurred words at the incarceration of white collar workers. Equality never exists in white collar crimes; only profit and power.

Standards set by society are interpretations made individually with stern acceptance of loose emotions.

War!

If in truth we can demeanor our country's symbols, our political adversaries, and our own president, then we have to stand back and realize how we were able to tell this in truth.

Our military has kept this nation's freedom; if not, how has it been so possible to be who we are?

War is the final anger in politics.

The day the protestors outnumber those in uniform is the day we live in tyranny.

Some of our soldiers are still our children. They're not yet old enough to vote or old enough to drink alcohol. A soldier is old enough to be used as a political statement and die, even if our statements are wrong or right. There is no such statement that one can be for the troops and not the war. The war is our troops, and they alone will win or lose.

War can never be made of plateaus of right or wrong. War is wrong, but when at war, it is kill or be killed. There is no place for humanity during war. There is only a place to win, so humanity can instill itself into freedom gained.

History will always have symbols, right or wrong. Without symbols, we have no history. There is the confederate flag of the southern states and the United States of America flag from the northern states. This is a fact of history. That is why there are so many graves to be tended.

Differences create opinions of differences which sometimes take men of opinions and peace to war.

It doesn't matter who fired the first shot. The only thing that matters is who is standing to clean the weapons and store them.

Soldiers who die in their belief of what they are fighting for are right. Society is only left to judge the wrong.

Protesting is said to be the best expression in freedom, but there is also dumb protesting which hurts the discords of true expression. There is always exaggeration in protesting, and that is always the voice that is heard.

War is always a last resort, but someday we have to wish for it. Freedom is that wish.

A commander and chief have many faces. The office of the presidency is above the position of the person. The person can only feebly stand within its shadow of grace.

One individual can make a difference; one nation can make that one individual.

Terrorism sounds like what is said. It can't be any other way because of the dead.

Peace is peace.

If all men could take their turn holding babies in the world while fighting, maybe we would not have war.

Does anyone question a soldier's religion as he goes into war to do his job? If no one questions a soldier, why do they concern themselves with what religion a presidential candidate might be?

Many books, many authors, or known political positions decry the rights and wrongs of war. Yet, the only true part of their position is the freedom they have to express that which is right or wrong after a war's outcome.

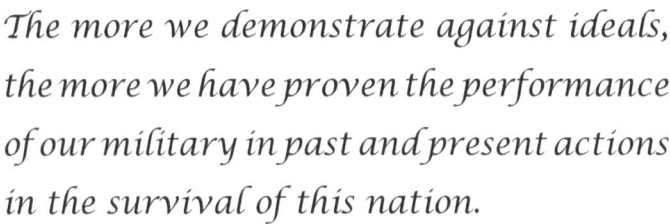

The more we demonstrate against ideals, the more we have proven the performance of our military in past and present actions in the survival of this nation.

The frustrations of being free are the emotions it brings in protecting what we feel.

Bend down and touch a dead soldier's grave, and then maybe a bond of freedom will be made. If not, then just walk away as you are free.

Shake a military man's or woman's hand,

and feel who you are to them, not who they are to you. (Why are you waiting?)

If freedom is so important to demonstrate for, then it must be important enough to fight and die for—period.

If your eyes are open to what you feel is right about war, then look behind them into your insight.

War is very terrible, but so is slavery. Just look at the Negro's history in this nation.

The smallest price to pay for freedom is to live it. The biggest price is to ignore it in its time of need.

You do not have to fight in war to protect freedom, but you do have to fight with a just reason to improve it, and make it right while you are at war.

As long as you have an enemy that threatens the foundation of your beliefs, you will always have an aggravation to war.

There is no way to demonstrate justly

for peace unless you surrender your own freedom and no one else's. Surrender the telephone you have, the friends you have, the house you live in, the TV you have, the TV programs you watch, the newspapers you read, the books that changed your mind, the car you drive, the friends you pal around with, the soap you wash with, the meals you love to eat, and the relatives you love and know. Don't run to Canada. They are our neighbors.

Media

We are not given the news today. We are told what it is. Not all is the media, so where is the real story? Is it just all an opinion?

The news media is the only profession that, when gathered to audit their own behavior, will find its faults in public opinion, and dissect it to prove their own right.

Religion dogs freedom of expression, while freedom of expression dogs religion as our Constitution barks at both of them.

Most editors today are the word police themselves. They are the entrepreneurs *of profit.*

Attitudes of bias have rubbed off from the editors of the news to the guy that sweeps their floors to pick up the scraps. The sweeper has a lifelong job.

Reporters were the backbone of the news. Now, they are nothing more than slipped discs of confusing information with unnamed sources.

During these times of war, it would seem the media has no sense of security or the meaning of propaganda. The news media gives up our dirty laundry no matter how big or small the load, and then the enemy dries it out to show the wrinkles to the embarrassment of our troops.

It's not how wrong or right the news is; it's the biased character of the news presented in the right and wrong.

Although news medias are not freedom, it gives us the insight to show the American freedoms even when it is done blindly.

If we live in a free and open society, why does the news hide people as unnamed sources to report freely what should be part of the facts?

Where did unnamed sources originate? Are they the giver of news, or the printer of the supposed facts?

Unnamed sources have become a convenience for the media to print with an attitude of bias without possible revocation to fact.

In today's news, unnamed sources are larceny at best.

How free are we in America when the media has to use an unnamed source for a voice in freedom?

Where in the Constitution does it say an unnamed source has the same rights as the news media?

How can the unnamed source hold a secret identity when the unnamed source becomes part of the news itself? The public has a right to know; so, how can the media say they are protected by the Constitution of these United States when the public has this right to know? Where does the person whose life and liberty that are exposed to open, unconfirmed innuendoes of guilt or innocence prior to the final proof go to if the protection of the Constitution has completely no meaning except for the media? What does "innocent until proven guilty" mean to the media?

Doesn't the Constitution say that man is considered innocent until proven guilty? Doesn't it also say that equality must be maintained until a jury of peers decides the guilt or innocence; thereafter all information becomes a matter of public record? Then why does the public need to know anything until all proof in the records is ready? Does it exist in stories not required to be public record that have the right under the Constitution to destroy a human being's status or way of life by using unnamed sources?

If there is bias in the news, and bias in the facts, whose freedom to know exists?

If the corporate news CEOs, editors, writers, and news columnists had their children in the military, would we be reading about the mistakes our soldiers make, and would we be reading in detail how they were made? Or, would it be a well-thought-out report?

It's time that the security and strength of this nation be shown at all times during any type of conflict. The written word can make that difference.

Responsible wording must fall upon our media without prejudice to fact.

The media can be considered to be the most responsible people toward investigation of our attitudes of freedoms.

The heartbeat of our Constitution is not the defining of written law alone. It's the words of our media in their interpretation of the facts toward the truth that is the heartbeat.

This nation cannot afford unnamed sources when it comes to our politics, our war activities, and our criminal justice court trials of guilt or innocence as it strikes at the foundation of equality for the right to know the truth!

Corporate

America

Corporate America must own some of our legislators. If not, look at banking loans and insurance loans. No one individual can get a full comprehensive credit report on a bank or loan company.

Corporations can file bankruptcy just to rename or reorganize. Can you, as an individual, do the same?

Corporations can produce an unsafe product that actually has killed, yet corporations admit to no faults, and the public loses its right to know.

If personal records can be made public after a conviction in a crime, why can't a corporation's records of fault in a faulty product case be made public? Even a personal divorce is a matter of public record. The Freedom of Information Act can pull up dirt on our government, but our laws hide corporate faults.

Health corporations pay high salaries to their CEOs—in the millions—yet the drug programs are supported by huge costs to the average senior citizen on a fixed income.

The average man's lifetime investments can be ripped off by CEOs of corporations. These actions destroy the average man's livelihood, retirement, and his capability to live. The mental burden to these individuals is worse than if a person walked up, stripped him naked, and shot him in the head. Yet, these CEOs, after destroying so many lives, are slapped on the hand and serve a few years in a homestyle prison. Does anyone go back to look at the lives they destroyed?

Our nation's pharmaceutical corporations' market pricing is outrageous, including the corporate HMOs, when it comes to the emotional stability and lives of our elderly with illnesses. A free market means not enslaving a nation's retirees with greed, but helping the old builders of this nation to realize a respectful ending of their lives; how disrespectful! Where is our leadership in Washington, D.C.? They gave some of these corporations' subsidies, which means our taxes. A new

Boston Tea Party may wake everybody up to this disgrace.

Shopping

Shopping at large, corporate department stores today is like going fishing.

When you catch a clerk by pure chance, they are uneducated to the system and the product. Most of the time they have an air about them that makes you want to throw them back like a bad fish catch.

Co-workers, friends, and the store clerk's cell phone are a customer's worst enemy. When trying to get service, they never know or seem to care if the customer is there.

Clerks cannot count correct change with or without a computer. Give them the difference in change to round off to the nearest figure and watch the panicked look on their faces.

●

Service centers for customers are an island of despair. During the holidays, or regular shopping days, the lines of customers are so long that the aisles in the department stores become human traffic jams. It could get to the point of exchanging a gift before you purchase it for the holiday or birthday.

●

When you are elderly and you have a question about the product or store procedures on sales, you are either treated like a child or patronized to a point of wanting to vomit. It would be better to *go fishing.*

If you want to call and complain about a product or service, the phone menu is longer than the lines at the customer service center.

Did you ever notice how fast you are informed about a recording of your conversation and how long it takes to get a conversation with someone?

Yesterday, in the good old days, a customer was always right.

Today, go fishing. They know there are a lot more fish like you in the sea to bait and hook.

Today, stores do not notify you if your order is in, if your repair is finished, or if your auto service is complete. You have to make the calls, as they don't want a bigger phone bill.

God

There are so many religions and only one God to believe in.

The second coming of Christ has already happened. It is in the heart and mind of those who believe. Only the sacrifice is missing. Man was given that benefit at the cross. Anything beyond this is biblical which was written by man.

Moral thoughts and actions are social handcuffs except in the belief of God.

Immoral actions are reprehensible against the good of man in the belief of God or not.

The nonbelievers and the atheists were born under God's freedoms. Their bibles are the moral writings of the Constitution of these United States. The question is how is it that the Constitution gives equality to both believers and atheists if it supposedly was written with the words of God involved?

To say there is life after death is to assume you can remember before you were!

Our Young

Too many reckless young people promote their own agenda in their media career when reporting our nation's actions in time of war.

Our strengths of this nation today are no longer in our young alone; it is in our greater generation of elderly. Both need each other in time of war.

Our young must be turned back toward our flag, our history, and our image of who we are as a nation, even if it means dismantling our education system as we know it today. Our politics must be put at balance in our education system.

Our young are being raised in a secular society image that is only good if the responsibility teaches them an understanding toward how we maintain our freedom.

A secular society has to understand itself when it creates reckless, arrogant, and disrespectful punks.

Today, it is too late to call for respect by our young while they beat our authority or maturity into the ground.

Strong discipline must be used today in the raising of our nation's young. We are on the path of losing them as we sit in apprehension of war and our freedoms.

Look at our schools. The students show more appeal and respect for Hollywood-style movies and the music industry than responsible life.

A car, a college, a bottle of booze, and sex do not make this a nation.

A lot of our prisons are more modern than our schools. Is this not going backwards?

In protecting our freedoms while in combat, our young soldiers eat K rations and sometimes less than that, while our criminals at home today eat steaks, enjoy holiday banquets, and cry about being mistreated. Is this justice or bias? Ask the ACLU.

Those who informed the parents, in the past and present, to let their kids do their own thing (such as don't spank them, and let the kids treat you as equal, or treat the kids as equal) must feel proud today. Look at our schools, our street crimes, the movies we have, our racial inequality, our national patriotism, and last, but not least, our image in the world. How great is it to do our own thing?

Our American image is crippled by irresponsible and reprehensible, selfish, and self-centered egotistical career-oriented young people who think power and the dollar are theirs to have at the expense of our nation's image. All this is for the heightening of their own personal career. Apparently, they lack grandparents from the greatest generation; or could it be a euphoric dream that their freedom will never be lost because they are Americans?

Get off the boat, young people; we're at war!

Young people should not act stupid,

as it reflects on those who are their grandparents; today, they may have directly raised you past their mistakes, but not the ones that bore you; the ones you are now acting like.

Patriotism

A patriot is one who loves his country and respects its authority, interests, and safety.

Patriotism is love for or devotion to one's country.

Patriotism can be elusive when it comes to freedom of expression.

Being patriotic can cost more than freedom of speech.

Patriotism in America is born and nurtured through participation of one's family in events of importance to one's country and acceptance of the family in its social standing.

If one is satisfied with his social standings, he can be very patriotic to his country. If not, he can become its enemy.

Patriotism is not words; it's actions upon the words spoken.

Being patriotic means taking words and acting with emotions of patriotism with them, for them, and on them.

When our forefathers signed the Constitution, they endured death, torture, loss of family members, and loss of property and wealth. Many died in poverty.

Our forefathers did not worry about the power of their party or how many terms they could serve.

Our forefathers did not worry about their pay or retirement benefits as they died for a free nation of equality.

Our forefathers, themselves, defined true patriotism.

Patriotism, for the well-positioned in our society, is a July 4 celebration. For those who are poor, it's maintaining the balance of power on the many battlefields of life in America. It's called poor educational bias and the ghetto.